What Every Parent Needs to Tell Their Children About Money

Crossing the Rubicon

Brian Connelly

Connelly Bitcoin Partners Press

Published by

PIKETOWN
PRESS

ISBN: 979-8-9961058-1-6

Opening

I still have my father's diploma.

MIT, 1947. He paid for it by washing test tubes at two dollars an hour.

A year at MIT in 1947 cost four hundred dollars. Two hundred hours of honest work. That was the deal.

Today a year at MIT costs sixty-two thousand dollars. That is more than a hundred and fifty times what it cost my father. The buildings are the same buildings. The professors are, on average, about as smart. What changed was not MIT. What changed was the dollar.

That is not a small change. That is a categorical collapse in what a dollar represents, and it happened inside two generations. It did not happen because MIT got better. It happened because the dollar got worse.

This book is about why, and what you need to tell your children about it, and what you can do about it before they inherit the bill.

I am a parent. I have four children. I have spent twenty years running a one-person consultancy through every market cycle and technology shift since the dial-up modem. I have watched institutional money up close, from inside the New York Stock Exchange, from inside General Electric Asset Management, from inside MIT itself, where I paid for a Bitcoin course in 2017 using Bitcoin. I am not an economist. I am not a politician. I am the person you talk to at the edge of a kid's birthday party, when the conversation turns, for the fourth time this year, to how nobody can afford anything anymore.

The conversation at that party is the right conversation. Most people are having it. Almost nobody has the framework to explain what they are feeling.

This book is the framework.

Part One

What money actually is

Chapter 1

Money is a technology, not a thing

In the early 1900s, a German ethnographer arrived on the island of Yap, in the western Pacific, and found something he did not expect. The islanders had money. It worked. People bought land with it, settled debts, arranged marriages. But the money was stone.

Limestone discs. Some of them twelve feet across, taller than the men who carved them. They sat in front of houses and along village paths, often half-buried in the ground. Nobody moved them. Nobody needed to. When a stone changed hands, when a debt was paid or a daughter's marriage arranged, the stone stayed exactly where it was. What moved was the knowledge of who owned it.

One famous stone sat at the bottom of the ocean. It had sunk during transport from a quarry on a neighboring island, more than two hundred miles across open water. The men who watched it go down came home and told the village what had happened. The village agreed: the stone still counted. Its owner was still rich. The stone's purchasing power was undiminished. It was money. It just happened to be underwater.

If that sounds ridiculous, hold the feeling for a moment. We will come back to it.

Most people, if you ask them what money is, will tell you it is a thing. Paper. Coin. A number on a screen. Something you earn, something you spend, something you either have or you don't.

That answer is wrong in a way that matters.

Money is not a thing. Money is a technology. It is a tool humans invented to solve a specific problem, the same way the wheel solves a specific problem and writing solves a specific problem. The wheel moves weight. Writing moves knowledge across time. Money moves value across space, across time, and between strangers who do not trust each other.

That last part, between strangers who do not trust each other, is the part most people miss. And it is the part that explains everything that has gone wrong.

Think about a world without money. Not as a utopia. As a logistics problem.

You raise chickens. Your neighbor grows wheat. You need wheat. He needs a new roof. You do not build roofs. The roofer needs shoes. The cobbler needs eggs, but not your eggs, because he already has too many. He needs goat milk, and the nearest goatherd is three towns over and wants lumber.

This is not a thought experiment. This is Tuesday, in any village, in any century before someone figured out money. Economists call it the double coincidence of wants. I call it a mess. You cannot run a civilization on barter any more than you can run a highway system on footpaths. It does not scale.

Money is what scales it. Money is the thing you accept not because you want it, but because someone else will. The chicken farmer takes the coin not because he can eat a coin, but because the roofer will take it. The roofer takes it because the cobbler will. The cobbler takes it because the goatherd will. The whole chain works not because any of them want the coin, but because all of them trust that the next person in the chain will accept it.

That is a technology. One of the most important ones humans ever built.

But not every technology works equally well. A bridge can be wood or steel. A record can be vinyl or digital. And money—real money, the kind that holds a civilization together for centuries instead of decades—needs three properties. Only three. Get all three right and the money works. Lose any one of them and the money fails. Sometimes slowly. Sometimes overnight.

The three properties are scarcity, verification, and memory.

Scarcity

If you can make more of it easily, it is not money. It is a receipt.

Gold works as money, has worked as money for five thousand years, partly because you cannot fake the supply. Gold is rare. Pulling it out of the earth is brutal, expensive, dangerous work. A Roman gold miner in Spain spent years in a tunnel cut by hand. A forty-niner in California froze in a river, pan in hand, for a few flakes a day. The difficulty is not a bug. The difficulty is the point. The cost of producing gold is what makes it trustworthy. If you could grow gold in a garden, nobody would accept it as payment.

Salt worked as money in East Africa and parts of China for the same reason. Not because salt is inherently precious (the ocean is full of it) but because in landlocked Ethiopia, getting salt to market meant a weeks-long caravan through desert. The journey was the cost. The cost was the proof.

The Yap islanders understood this instinctively. Their limestone discs were not carved from local rock. They were quarried on Palau, an island more than two hundred miles across open ocean, then loaded onto bamboo rafts and sailed home. Men died making that crossing. The size of the stone and the danger of the journey were the whole point. A stone that anyone could carve in an afternoon, from rock in the next field, would have been worth nothing.

Scarcity is not about rarity for its own sake. It is about cost. Real cost: in labor, in time, in risk. If the thing can be produced cheaply, it can be debased cheaply. And if it can be debased cheaply, someone will. This is not cynicism. It is history. Every government that has ever controlled a money supply has eventually expanded it. Every single one.

We will get to that.

Verification

It is not enough for money to be scarce. You have to be able to prove it is scarce. You have to be able to check.

Gold passes this test beautifully. Gold is dense, denser than almost anything you could try to substitute. Archimedes figured this out in a bathtub in the third century BC, when he realized that a gold crown and a fake crown of the same weight would displace different amounts of water. He reportedly ran through the streets naked, shouting about it. The physics is elegant but the point is simple: you can test gold. Bite it. Weigh it. Drop it in water. Scratch it on a touchstone. A merchant in Constantinople in the year 900 and a pawnbroker in Newark in 2024 use essentially the same tests, because gold is gold. It does not lie about what it is.

Shells are harder. Cowrie shells worked as money across Africa and South Asia for centuries, partly because the specific species used, small, smooth, nearly impossible to counterfeit by hand, was naturally verifiable. You could look at it and know. But when European traders figured out they could harvest cowries by the shipload from the Maldives and flood African markets, the system broke. The supply was no longer what it appeared to be. Verification failed because the thing being verified, scarcity, had been destroyed from the outside.

A dollar bill is easy to verify as a dollar bill. Hold it up to the light, check the watermark, feel the cotton paper. But verifying that it is a dollar bill is not the same as verifying that it is worth a dollar. Those are two different questions, and most people never think to ask the second one.

Memory

The hardest problem money solves is not scarcity and not verification. It is memory.

Who owns what? Who paid whom? Who still owes? In a village of fifty people, you can keep track in your head. In a city of fifty thousand, you cannot. In a country of three hundred and thirty million, the question of who owns what is an engineering problem of staggering complexity, and the answer to that problem is a ledger.

Every monetary system in history is, at bottom, a ledger. The Yap islanders kept theirs in oral memory: the whole village remembered who owned which stone, and when ownership changed, the whole village updated the record. Nobody wrote it down. Nobody needed to. The community was the ledger.

That system works when your economy is an island. It does not work when your economy is a continent.

So civilizations scaled the ledger. Clay tablets in Mesopotamia. Paper records in Song Dynasty China. Double-entry bookkeeping in Renaissance Venice, a technology so important that Goethe called it one of the finest inventions of the human mind, and he was not exaggerating. Each advance in ledger technology allowed money to travel further, faster, between more strangers.

But every one of those ledgers has a problem. Someone has to keep it. And whoever keeps the ledger can change it.

A king can debase a coin. A bank can lend out money it does not have. A government can print currency until the paper is worth more as kindling than as cash. These are not hypothetical failures. They are the main plot of monetary history. Rome did it. Henry VIII did it. The Continental Congress did it. The Weimar Republic did it. We are doing it now.

The ledger is the vulnerability. Not because ledgers are bad, but because centralized ledgers are corruptible. And humans, given the power to edit a ledger in their own favor, will eventually do exactly that. That is not an insult. It is an observation. It is what you see when you look at five thousand years of monetary history without flinching.

So here is the scorecard. Money that actually works—money you can build a life on and hand to your children with a straight face—needs three things.

It needs to be scarce, so it cannot be conjured out of thin air. It needs to be verifiable, so you can tell the real from the fake. And it needs a ledger that no one can corrupt, so the record of who owns what stays honest even when the people keeping it would prefer otherwise.

For most of human history, gold came closest. Scarce, verifiable, beautiful, durable. But gold's ledger was always centralized: in vaults, in banks, in governments. And governments, over and over, broke the promise. Clipped the coins. Suspended convertibility. Printed paper against gold that was not there.

The technology of money has been trying to solve the ledger problem for five thousand years. The scarcity problem and the verification problem were solved by nature: by the physical properties of gold, by the impossibility of faking what the earth made rare. But the ledger problem was always a human problem, and humans kept failing it.

Remember the stone at the bottom of the ocean? The one the village agreed still counted? That system worked because everyone on Yap knew the truth and nobody had the power to change it. The whole village was the ledger, and no single person could edit it.

Hold that thought. We are going to need it.

That is where the story of this book begins to turn. But before we get there, we need to understand exactly how the ledger broke. Not in theory, but in practice, with names and dates and numbers you can verify yourself.

That is the next chapter.

Chapter 2

How money gets real

The quarry was on Palau. The money was needed on Yap. Between the two lay more than two hundred miles of open Pacific: no navigation instruments, no engine, no coast guard.

The men who made the crossing did it on bamboo rafts. They sailed to Palau, spent weeks or months in limestone caves carving a disc, sometimes five feet across, sometimes ten, and then they lashed it to the raft and sailed home. Some of them did not make it home.

The ones who did arrived with something everyone on Yap understood immediately: proof. Not proof that the stone was pretty. Not proof that the stone was rare. Proof that someone had paid for it: in labor, in danger, in months of life they would not get back. The stone was valuable because the work was real. The work was real because it could not be faked.

That is how money gets real. Not by declaration. Not by law. By cost.

There is a phrase that will matter later in this book: “proof of work.” It comes from the world of Bitcoin, but Bitcoin did not invent the idea. Bitcoin named it. The idea is as old as money itself.

Proof of work means: the thing you are using as money carries evidence of what it cost to produce. The cost is not incidental. The cost is the message. When a Yap islander looked at a twelve-foot limestone disc, he was not admiring the craftsmanship. He was reading a receipt. That stone said: someone crossed an ocean, someone spent months in a cave with hand tools, someone risked drowning on the way home. You cannot lie about that. You cannot shortcut it. The stone carries its own proof.

Gold says the same thing, in a different language. Nobody stamps a gold coin with a label explaining that it took thousands of tons of crushed rock, processed over weeks, to produce a single ounce. But the label is unnecessary. The scarcity of gold in the earth’s crust is the label. The reason gold is heavy in your hand is the same reason it is heavy to produce. The weight is the work. The work is the trust.

This is the part most explanations of money skip past. They will tell you that money needs to be scarce, and that is true. They will tell you that money needs to be durable and portable and divisible, and that is true too. But they rarely explain what those properties are actually producing.

They are producing trust.

Not the kind of trust you have in a friend. Not the kind of trust you extend when you shake hands on a deal. This is a different species of trust: impersonal, mathematical, verifiable by anyone. When you hold a gold coin, you are holding the compressed labor of miners, smelters, and assayers. You do not need to trust the person who gave it to you. You do not need to know his name. The coin speaks for itself because the work that produced it speaks for itself.

That is a profound thing, if you stop to think about it. Money, at its best, is a machine for creating trust between strangers. The baker in medieval Florence did not know the wool merchant who walked into his shop. He did not need to. The gold florin the merchant placed on the counter carried its own credentials. Scarce. Dense. Tested by fire. The coin said: someone, somewhere, did the work. And the baker believed the coin because the coin could not lie.

Here is where it gets uncomfortable.

What happens when you remove the work?

A gold coin is heavy because gold is rare and hard to extract. A dollar bill weighs about one gram. The paper costs roughly six cents to print. The difference between a hundred-dollar bill and a one-dollar bill is not material—it is the number printed on the front. Same paper. Same ink. Same weight. The hundred is worth a hundred because the government says so.

That is a fundamentally different technology. It is not proof of work. It is proof of authority. The bill does not carry evidence of what it cost to produce, because what it cost to produce is trivial. It carries a promise: the United States government guarantees that this piece of paper is worth one hundred dollars. The cost of breaking that promise is supposed to be so high (economic collapse, loss of global reserve status, political catastrophe) that the promise functions as a substitute for the work.

For a while, that substitution held. The dollar was backed by gold until 1971. The promise was: bring us your paper, we will give you gold. You could verify the promise by asking for the gold. Some people did. Charles de Gaulle actually sent a warship to pick up France's gold from the Federal Reserve in the 1960s. He did not trust the promise. He wanted the metal.

In 1971, Nixon closed the gold window. No more exchanges. The promise changed from "this paper represents gold" to "this paper represents our word." The work was gone. The authority remained.

We have been running on authority ever since.

I want to be careful here, because this is the point where most books about money become political, and I have no interest in writing a political book. I am writing a book about physics.

Not literal physics. The physics of trust. The mechanics of how value gets created, verified, and remembered across a civilization. Those mechanics have rules, the same way a bridge has rules. You can build a bridge out of anything: wood, stone, steel, cable. But the bridge has to hold weight. If you ignore the physics, the bridge falls. It does not fall because the builder was a bad person. It falls because the load exceeded the capacity.

The physics of money says: trust that rests on work is more durable than trust that rests on authority. Not because authority is always corrupt. Not because governments are always evil. But because authority can change its mind, and work cannot. The gold that was mined in the Roman Empire is still gold. The coins that Rome debased, clipped, shaved, diluted with base metals, told the whole story of an empire that needed to spend more than it earned. The coins did not lie. The emperor lied. The coins just recorded it.

There is a word that captures this idea, and it is an old word: honest.

Honest money is money that tells the truth about what it cost. A gold coin is honest. A Yap stone is honest. A salt bar carried across the Ethiopian desert is honest. Each one says: this is what I cost. Check if you want. The cost is baked in.

Dishonest money is money that claims to be worth more than it cost to produce. A clipped Roman denarius was dishonest. A Continental dollar, printed by the Congress in 1775 with nothing behind it, was dishonest. The phrase "not worth a Continental" survived in American English for two centuries because Americans remembered what happened when the government printed money without the work to back it.

I am not using "honest" and "dishonest" as moral judgments. I am using them the way an engineer uses "sound" and "unsound." A sound bridge holds. An unsound bridge might hold for a while, years, even decades, but the physics is wrong, and eventually the physics wins.

The physics always wins.

Here is what I want you, as a parent, to take from this chapter before we move forward.

When your child asks you what money is, and they will, the answer is not "it's what you use to buy things." That is like saying a bridge is "what you use to cross a river." It is true, but it tells you nothing about whether the bridge will hold.

The answer is: money is a technology for storing and transferring trust. The best versions of that technology are the ones where the trust is built into the thing itself: where the cost is real, the proof is visible, and nobody has the power to change the ledger. The worst versions are the ones where the trust depends entirely on a promise from someone with every incentive to break it.

The money in your wallet right now is the second kind. The money your parents used was backed by the first kind, until 1971. The money your grandparents used was the first kind.

Three generations. That is how fast this changed.

Your children are growing up inside that change, and most of them will never be told that it happened. Unless you tell them. That is what this book is for.

The Yap islanders did not have a word for proof of work. They did not need one. The ocean was the proof. The months in the quarry were the proof. The risk of drowning was the proof. Everyone on the island knew what a stone cost, because everyone on the island had watched someone pay it.

What the islanders had, without naming it, was something modern economies have lost: a money supply that could not be inflated by anyone, no matter how powerful. The chief could not carve a new stone in his backyard. The strongest man on the island could not wish one into existence. The supply was governed by the physics of limestone and the geography of the Pacific Ocean.

That was not a limitation. That was the feature.

The next chapter is about what happened when civilizations decided the limitation was the problem.

Chapter 3

How money stays real

For six hundred years, the English government kept its accounts on sticks.

Hazelwood, specifically. A notch was carved for each transaction: a wide notch for a pound, a narrow notch for a shilling, a nick for a penny. Then the stick was split lengthwise. The government kept one half. The taxpayer kept the other. If there was ever a dispute, the two halves were matched. If the notches lined up, the record was true. If they didn't, someone was lying.

The system was called the Exchequer tally. It worked for six centuries. It was not elegant. It was not sophisticated. It was wood.

In 1834, Parliament finally decided to get rid of the old tallies. They had switched to paper ledgers decades earlier, and the basement of the Palace of Westminster was full of six hundred years' worth of surplus sticks. Someone decided to burn them. They loaded the sticks into the furnaces beneath the House of Lords, stoked the fire, and went home.

The fire got out. It burned down the Palace of Westminster. Both chambers of Parliament—destroyed. The most powerful legislature in the world, incinerated by its own bookkeeping.

Charles Dickens, who watched the fire from across the Thames, later called it the most spectacular example of government mismanagement he had ever seen. He was not exaggerating by much.

I tell that story because it contains, in miniature, everything this chapter is about.

The tally stick was a ledger. A physical, tamper-evident, decentralized ledger. Both parties held a copy. Neither could alter their half without it failing to match the other. The system did not rely on trust between the parties. It relied on the physical properties of split wood. The grain of the hazelwood was the verification. The matching halves were the memory.

Six hundred years. Think about that. England went through the Crusades, the Black Death, the Wars of the Roses, the Reformation, the Civil War, and the Glorious Revolution, and the tally stick survived all of it. Not because it was the best technology. Because it solved the right problem.

The right problem is: who keeps the books?

This question sounds administrative. It is not. It is the question on which every economy in history has risen or fallen. Who records the transactions? Who remembers the debts? Who has the authority to say "this happened" or "this didn't"? And—the question that matters most—who can change the record after the fact?

In a village, the answer is simple: everyone remembers. The Yap islanders did not need a bank. They did not need a treasury. They did not need an accountant. The village was the ledger. When a stone changed hands, the village remembered. There was no record to forge because the record was the collective memory of everyone who lived there.

This works beautifully at small scale. It does not work at large scale. A city of ten thousand people cannot remember who owns which stone. A nation of three hundred million cannot remember who deposited what in which account. The records have to be written down, and the moment they are written down, someone has to write them.

That someone is the bookkeeper. And the bookkeeper is the single point of failure in every centralized monetary system ever built.

I do not mean that every bookkeeper is corrupt. Most are not. I mean that the position of bookkeeper creates a specific kind of power, the power to edit reality, and that power, across enough time and enough pressure, will be abused. Not because bookkeepers are bad people. Because the incentives are wrong.

Think about it from the bookkeeper's perspective. You are a medieval goldsmith in London. People bring you their gold for safekeeping. You issue receipts. The receipts begin to circulate as money. It is easier to hand someone a piece of paper than to haul gold across town. You realize, after a while, that nobody comes to collect all the gold at once. Most of it just sits in your vault.

So you start lending it out. You issue more receipts than you have gold. The extra receipts circulate just like the real ones. Nobody can tell the difference. You collect interest on the loans. You are, in a very real sense, creating money out of nothing: out of the gap between the gold you hold and the receipts you have issued.

This is not a hypothetical. This is the origin of fractional reserve banking. It was invented by goldsmiths in seventeenth-century London, and it spread to every banking system in the world. It works as long as everyone does not ask for their gold at the same time. When they do, it is called a bank run, and the bookkeeper's lie is exposed.

The goldsmith was the ledger keeper. The power to keep the ledger was the power to inflate the money supply. That power was not granted by any law or constitution. It emerged from the structure of the system itself, as naturally as water finds the lowest point.

Every advance in ledger technology has made this problem bigger, not smaller.

Clay tablets in Mesopotamia kept records of grain debts. The temple priests who maintained those records were the first central bankers: they decided how much grain was owed, how much interest was due, and when debts were forgiven. The tablets were accurate, until they were not. Priests had their own debts, their own allies, their own politics.

Paper ledgers in China enabled the first paper money: promissory notes issued by the Song Dynasty government in the tenth century. For a while, the notes were backed by metal. Then the government needed to fund a war. Then another war. Then another. The printing accelerated. The money lost its value. By the end of the Yuan Dynasty, the paper was worthless.

Double-entry bookkeeping in Renaissance Venice was a genuine breakthrough: every transaction recorded twice, once as a debit and once as a credit. The two columns had to balance. If they did not, someone had made an error or committed a fraud. It was the tally stick principle scaled up: two records that had to match. But both records were in the same book, kept by the same person. The tamper resistance was theoretical. The power was concentrated.

Here is the pattern, and I want you to see it clearly, because it repeats in every chapter that follows.

A civilization needs money. Money needs a ledger. The ledger starts honest: stone, wood, clay, matched copies, checks and balances. The system works. The economy grows. The growth creates pressure: wars to fund, debts to service, promises to keep. The pressure lands on the ledger keeper. The ledger keeper adjusts the record. A little at first. Then more. Then much more. The money loses its meaning. The civilization either reforms or collapses.

Rome. China. England. France. The United States.

The specific details change. The pattern does not.

What made the tally stick work for six hundred years was not the wood. It was the split. Both parties held a copy. Neither could alter the record alone. The system distributed the memory so that no single party controlled it.

What made the Yap stones work was the same principle: the whole village was the ledger. No individual, no chief, no priest had the authority to edit the record. The memory was distributed across every person on the island.

What makes centralized ledgers fail, eventually, is the opposite: one party controls the record. And that party, under enough pressure, will change it.

The question that has haunted money for five thousand years is: can you build a ledger that scales beyond a village but cannot be corrupted by the people who run it?

For most of history, the answer was no. The best you could do was build checks and balances: split the tally, require two signatures, audit the books. But checks and balances are administered by people, and people can be pressured, bribed, or overruled by someone with more authority.

The answer, for five thousand years, was always no. You cannot build an incorruptible ledger at civilizational scale.

Until very recently.

But that part of the story comes later. First, we need to watch the pattern play out. With specific names, specific dates, and specific numbers. Because the pattern is not abstract. It has a body count.

That is Part Two.

Part Two

How we got here

Chapter 4

The long history, briefly

If you hold a Roman denarius from the reign of Augustus, around the time of Christ, it weighs about three and a half grams. It is nearly pure silver. It feels like a coin should feel: solid, heavy for its size, honest in the hand.

If you hold a denarius from two hundred and fifty years later, the reign of Gallienus, near the end, it weighs about the same. But it is not the same. The silver is mostly gone. What you are holding is a bronze coin with a thin wash of silver on the surface, like a lie wearing a good suit. Rub it between your fingers and the silver comes off.

That progression, from honest coin to plated fraud, took about two and a half centuries. It did not happen by accident. It happened because Rome needed to pay for things it could not afford, and the men who controlled the mint discovered that you could stretch the money supply by reducing the silver content of each coin. A little less each year. A little less each decade. So gradually that no single emperor seemed responsible.

By the time Diocletian took power in 284 AD, the denarius contained less than five percent of the silver it had carried under Augustus. Prices had risen by a factor of a thousand. Soldiers, who were paid in debased coins, demanded more coins. The government minted more coins. The coins bought less. The soldiers demanded more. The spiral had its own gravity.

Diocletian's response was to issue the Edict on Maximum Prices, a law that fixed the price of over a thousand goods and services, from wheat to haircuts, with the death penalty for anyone who charged more. It did not work. You cannot fix prices when the money itself is broken. The merchants stopped selling. The markets emptied. The economy did not recover. Rome did not fall because of barbarians at the gate. Rome fell because the coins in the soldiers' pockets were worth less every year, and eventually the soldiers stopped showing up.

I could fill a book with Rome alone. I will not. The point is the pattern, and the pattern is simple enough that you can explain it to your child at the dinner table.

A government controls the money. The money starts honest. The government needs to spend more than it collects: for wars, for roads, for bread and circuses, for whatever the population demands or the rulers desire. The government cannot raise taxes fast enough, or high enough, without provoking revolt. So it does the quiet thing instead. It debases the money. A little at a time. Slowly enough that most people do not notice, at least not at first.

By the time they notice, the damage is structural. Savings are worth less. Wages buy less. Prices rise. The people who are closest to the new money, the government, the military, the connected, spend it first, before the prices adjust. The people who are furthest from the new money—the farmers, the laborers, the shopkeepers, the parents—absorb the loss. The wealth transfers upward. It always transfers upward.

This is not a conspiracy theory. It is a mechanism. It has a name: the Cantillon effect, after Richard Cantillon, who described it in the 1730s. New money benefits whoever touches it first and hurts whoever touches it last. It is as predictable as gravity, and just as impersonal.

Henry VIII understood this mechanism perfectly, even if he never read Cantillon.

In 1544, Henry needed money. He always needed money: six wives, a break with Rome, a navy, a court that expected to live lavishly. Parliament would not grant him enough taxes. So he did what the Roman emperors had done: he debased the currency.

The operation was called the Great Debasement, and the name is earned. Over four years, from 1544 to 1551 (Henry started it, his son Edward VI continued it), the silver content of English coins was reduced from ninety-two percent to twenty-five percent. The government melted down honest coins and re-minted them with cheaper metal. The profit went to the Crown.

The people of England had a phrase for what happened. They said the king's face was blushing. Because as the silver content dropped and the copper content rose, the coins turned reddish, and the part that turned red first was the raised surface, the king's nose on the portrait. Henry VIII became known as "Old Coppernose." It was not a term of affection.

Prices doubled in a decade. The poor suffered. The merchants who traded internationally, who knew what English coins were actually worth on the continent, demanded more of them. England's credit abroad collapsed. It took Elizabeth I, Henry's daughter, to repair the damage. In 1560 she ordered a full recoinage, pulling in the debased coins, melting them down, and issuing honest ones. It was expensive. It was painful. It worked. But it only worked because Elizabeth was willing to do the hard thing, and the hard thing was admitting that the coins her father had issued were lies.

The American colonies learned the same lesson the hard way.

When the Continental Congress needed to fund the Revolutionary War, it did not have the power to tax. That power belonged to the states, and the states were not eager to share it. So the Congress printed money—Continental dollars, backed by nothing but the promise of a government that did not yet fully exist.

The first printing, in 1775, was modest. By 1779, Congress had printed over two hundred million dollars in Continentals. Prices rose by a factor of a hundred. A bushel of corn that cost a dollar in 1776 cost a hundred dollars by 1779. Soldiers used the bills to wallpaper their barracks. Shopkeepers refused them. The phrase “not worth a Continental” entered the language and stayed there for two centuries.

George Washington himself wrote that a wagon of money could barely buy a wagon of provisions. He was not being poetic. He was being precise.

The experience burned so deeply that when the Founders wrote the Constitution, they included a clause, Article I, Section 10, that prohibited states from making “any Thing but gold and silver Coin a Tender in Payment of Debts.” They had lived through monetary collapse. They wanted to make sure nobody who came after them could do it again.

That lasted about a hundred and twenty years.

I am moving through this history quickly on purpose. If you want the full story of Roman monetary policy or the Great Debasement or the Continental dollar, there are excellent books. I will list them at the end. What I need you to see right now is the shape of the thing.

The shape is always the same. A government controls the money. The money starts honest. The government faces a crisis: a war, a famine, a political emergency. The crisis creates pressure to spend. The spending exceeds the income. The gap gets filled by debasing the money. The debasement transfers wealth from the people who hold the money to the people who control the money. The transfer is invisible to most people until it is too late.

Rome. England. America. China. France, twice if you count both John Law's Mississippi scheme in 1720 and the assignats of the French Revolution. Spain, under Philip II. Weimar Germany. Argentina. Zimbabwe. Venezuela.

The list is not short. The pattern is not subtle. And the pattern has a quality that should concern every parent reading this book: it accelerates.

Rome's debasement took two hundred and fifty years. Henry VIII accomplished his in four. The Continental dollar collapsed in five. The next chapter covers two dates, 1913 and 1971, that set the stage for a debasement so large and so fast that most Americans have not yet understood what happened.

The coins are not turning red this time. There is no copper showing through. But the purchasing power of the dollar has lost more than ninety-five percent of its value since 1913, and the mechanism is the same one that turned Henry's coins to copper and Rome's silver to bronze.

The pattern does not care what century it is. It does not care what language you speak or what flag you salute. It runs on the same physics every time: if the people who control the money can create more of it, they will. And the cost will be paid by the people who cannot.

That is the long history. Here is the short one.

Chapter 5

1913 and 1971

In 1913, a dollar bought what a dollar bought. That sounds like a tautology. It is not. It is a statement about the world your great-grandparents lived in.

A gallon of milk cost about thirty-six cents. A loaf of bread cost a nickel. A three-bedroom house in a decent neighborhood cost about three thousand dollars. A man working a factory job earned about seven hundred and fifty dollars a year, and that was enough to feed a family, pay rent, put something aside, and not feel like the ground was shifting underneath him.

The dollar had held roughly steady for a century. There were fluctuations, prices rose during wars, fell during panics, but the baseline held. A dollar in 1813 bought approximately what a dollar bought in 1913. That is a hundred years of monetary stability. Your great-grandmother did not worry about inflation. The word barely existed in common speech. Money held its value because money was gold, or redeemable for gold, and nobody could print gold.

Then two things happened. They are the two most important dates in American monetary history, and most Americans have never been taught either one.

The first date is December 23, 1913.

Congress was mostly out of town for Christmas. Woodrow Wilson signed the Federal Reserve Act into law. The United States got a central bank.

The arguments for the Federal Reserve were reasonable. The country had suffered a brutal financial panic in 1907: banks failed, depositors lost savings, the stock market dropped nearly fifty percent. The economy needed a lender of last resort, a backstop, an institution that could inject liquidity when the private banking system seized up. J.P. Morgan, the man, not the bank, had personally bailed out the system in 1907, and the general consensus was that relying on one wealthy man's judgment was not a sustainable arrangement.

So Congress created the Fed. A central bank with the power to issue currency, set interest rates, and regulate the banking system. The dollar would remain backed by gold. The Fed's role was stabilization, not money creation.

That was the promise.

Here is what happened.

In 1913, the total money supply of the United States, all the dollars in circulation and in bank accounts, was about thirteen billion dollars. By 1929, it had nearly doubled. By 1971, it had grown to about seven hundred billion. By 2008, it was nearly eight trillion. Today it is above twenty-one trillion.

That is not stabilization. That is expansion. Relentless, compounding, exponential expansion.

The Fed did not set out to debase the dollar. No institution ever does. But the Fed had the power to create money, and every crisis, the First World War, the Second World War, the Korean War, Vietnam, the oil shocks, the savings and loan crisis, the dot-com crash, 2008, COVID, created pressure to use that power. Each crisis was real. Each intervention was justified at the time. And each intervention expanded the money supply permanently, because the money that was created for the crisis was never withdrawn after the crisis ended.

There is always a next crisis. Tariffs. Sanctions. Wars that never quite end. Countries quietly moving their reserves out of dollars. Whatever name it carries when you read this sentence, the machine responds the same way: more money, created faster, to manage a problem that was caused by creating money too fast the last time.

The ratchet turns in one direction only. That is the physics of central banking.

For the first fifty-eight years of the Fed's existence, there was still a constraint. The dollar was backed by gold. Not perfectly, the ratio had been adjusted, the rules had been bent, but the fundamental promise remained: the United States government would exchange dollars for gold at a fixed rate. Foreign governments could show up at the Treasury with dollars and walk out with metal.

That promise was the leash. As long as it existed, the Fed could expand the money supply, but not without limit. At some point, the gold would run out, and someone would ask for it.

Someone did.

In the 1960s, France, under Charles de Gaulle, began exchanging its dollar reserves for gold. De Gaulle did not trust the United States to honor the promise indefinitely. He had watched the money supply grow. He had done the math. He sent a warship to New York to collect France's gold from the Federal Reserve Bank. Other countries followed.

The gold was leaving. The promise was becoming expensive to keep. And on August 15, 1971, Richard Nixon made a decision that changed everything.

The second date is August 15, 1971.

Nixon went on television on a Sunday evening, preempting the most popular show in America, which happened to be Bonanza, and announced what he called a "temporary" suspension of the dollar's convertibility into gold.

Temporary. That word matters. Nixon did not say he was abandoning the gold standard. He said he was suspending it: a pause, not a policy. A measure to defend the dollar against "international money speculators," which was his phrase for the foreign governments who were doing exactly what the system entitled them to do: exchanging paper for metal.

The suspension was never lifted. Fifty-five years later, it is still "temporary."

What Nixon did, in plain language, was remove the last physical constraint on money creation. Before August 15, 1971, the dollar was a claim on gold. After August 15, 1971, the dollar was a claim on the full faith and credit of the United States government, which is another way of saying it was a claim on a promise.

The leash was off.

I want to be precise about what changed, because the change is often described in ways that make it sound technical or obscure. It is neither.

Before 1971, if the government wanted to spend money it did not have, it faced a constraint: the gold supply. You can print paper dollars, but you cannot print gold. The gold in the vault set the boundary. Cross it, and the lie would be exposed when someone came to collect.

After 1971, the constraint was gone. The government could spend whatever it chose to spend, fund it by issuing debt, and the Federal Reserve could buy that debt by creating new dollars. No gold required. No vault to check. No physical limit of any kind.

This is not a Republican observation or a Democratic observation. Both parties have used this power enthusiastically. Every president since Nixon has presided over a growing money supply and a growing national debt. The disagreements between the parties are about what to spend the money on, not whether to create it.

The money gets created. That is the one thing both sides agree on, even when they agree on nothing else.

Here is what the removal of the constraint has meant in practice.

In 1971, the national debt of the United States was about four hundred billion dollars. Today it is approaching thirty-nine trillion. That number is so large that it has lost its ability to shock, so let me put it differently.

The debt increases by roughly seven and a half billion dollars every day. That is about eighty-eight thousand dollars per second. While you have been reading this chapter, the debt has grown by several million dollars. It will grow by several million more before you finish the next one.

Interest payments on the debt have now crossed one trillion dollars per year. That is more than the United States spends on its entire military. The country is paying more to service its past borrowing than it pays to defend itself. That is not a political talking point. It is a line item in the federal budget. You can look it up.

And the dollar, the unit of account in which all of this is measured, has lost more than ninety-five percent of its purchasing power since the Fed was created in 1913. The gallon of milk that cost thirty-six cents in 1913 costs about four dollars today. The house that cost three thousand dollars costs over four hundred thousand. My father's MIT tuition, four hundred dollars in 1947, is now sixty-two thousand.

The buildings are the same buildings.

I am not telling you this to make you angry. Anger is easy and it fades quickly. I am telling you this because you are a parent, and your children are going to inherit this, and if you do not understand how it works, you cannot explain it to them. And if you cannot explain it to them, they will absorb the consequences without ever understanding the cause.

The cause is simple. In 1913, we gave a small group of people the power to create money. In 1971, we removed the last constraint on that power. The money supply expanded. The purchasing power of each dollar declined. The wealth transferred—slowly, invisibly, relentlessly—from the people who earned and saved dollars to the people who created and borrowed them.

That is not a theory. That is arithmetic.

The next chapter is about what happened after 1971, particularly in 2008, when the arithmetic stopped being invisible and the bill started coming due.

Chapter 6

2008 and after

On September 15, 2008, a Monday, Lehman Brothers filed for bankruptcy. It was the largest bankruptcy in American history. Six hundred and thirty-nine billion dollars in assets—gone. Not slowly. Not over years. Over a weekend.

If you were a parent in 2008, you remember what came next. Not the financial details. Most people did not understand the financial details, and the people who did understand them were terrified. What you remember is the feeling. The feeling that the system, whatever the system was, had stopped working. Your 401(k) lost a third of its value. Maybe half. The news showed people lined up outside banks. The word "bailout" entered your kitchen vocabulary. Your neighbor lost his house. Maybe you almost lost yours.

What most people did not understand, what most people still do not understand, is what happened behind the closed doors, and why it matters more than anything else in this book.

Here is what happened, in plain language.

For decades, banks had been lending money to people who could not pay it back. They did this on purpose. Not because bankers are stupid, they are not, but because the system was structured so that it did not matter if the borrower paid it back. The bank made the loan, collected a fee, packaged the loan with thousands of other loans, and sold the package to investors. The risk moved. The fee stayed.

The investors who bought those packages, pension funds, insurance companies, foreign governments, were told the packages were safe. The credit rating agencies, the companies whose entire job was to assess risk, rated them AAA. The highest possible grade. As safe as US government debt.

They were not safe. They were backed by mortgages that were already defaulting. When enough of them defaulted at once, the packages became worthless, and the institutions holding them became insolvent. Not illiquid—insolvent. The money was gone.

The system did not have a word for what happened next, so I will supply one: the bookkeeper panicked.

The Federal Reserve and the US Treasury, the bookkeepers of the American economy, faced a choice. They could let the insolvent institutions fail. Banks would close. Depositors would lose money. The credit markets would freeze. The economy would crash hard, and it would take years to recover. People would suffer. Some of them would lose everything.

Or they could create money.

They created money.

The numbers are worth understanding, because they represent the largest single expansion of the money supply in American history. Until the next one.

The Troubled Asset Relief Program, TARP, authorized seven hundred billion dollars in direct government spending to purchase the toxic assets that nobody else would buy. The Federal Reserve, separately, created over a trillion dollars through a program called quantitative easing, a term that means, in plain English, "the central bank creates new dollars and uses them to buy financial assets." The Fed bought bonds. It bought mortgage-backed securities, the same ones that had just blown up. It bought them not because they were good investments but because buying them injected new money into the system, and the system was dying.

Between 2008 and 2014, the Federal Reserve's balance sheet, the total value of everything it had purchased with newly created money, grew from about nine hundred billion dollars to over four trillion. The Fed had more than quadrupled the monetary base in six years.

Nobody voted on this. No ballot measure. No constitutional amendment. The Fed has the authority to create money. It used that authority. The decision was made by a handful of people in a room, and the cost was distributed across every person who held dollars, which is not just every person in this country. Roughly forty percent of US dollars circulate outside American borders. The farmer in Colombia, the merchant in Nigeria, the factory worker in Vietnam who keeps his savings in dollars because his own currency is worse. They absorbed the debasement too. Nobody asked them. Nobody had to.

I want to pause here and say something that might sound like I am defending the decision. I am not defending it. I am not attacking it either. I am describing the mechanics.

The people who made these decisions were not villains. Many of them were genuinely terrified that the alternative, letting the system collapse, would cause suffering on a scale not seen since the Great Depression. They may have been right. A full financial collapse would have wiped out savings, frozen credit, and thrown millions of people out of work overnight. The bailout prevented that. In the short term, it worked.

But in the long term, it did something else. It proved, to the banks, to the markets, to the government itself, that the constraint was gone. Not just the gold constraint, which had been gone since 1971. The political constraint. The social constraint. The idea that there was some limit, some line, some amount of money creation that was too much.

There was no line. 2008 proved it. And once everyone knew there was no line, the behavior changed.

The banks that were bailed out in 2008 did not get smaller. They got bigger. The six largest banks in the

United States are larger today than they were before the crisis. Too big to fail became bigger than ever.

The Federal Reserve did not unwind its balance sheet. It could not. Selling the assets it had purchased would have crashed the markets it had just rescued. So the balance sheet stayed bloated. When the economy faltered again, the Fed expanded it further. It became the new normal.

And then COVID arrived.

In March 2020, the Federal Reserve created more money in a single quarter than it had created in the first ninety-five years of its existence. The balance sheet went from about four trillion to nearly nine trillion in less than two years. Congress passed stimulus bills totaling over five trillion dollars. Checks were mailed directly to households. The money supply exploded.

Prices followed. By 2022, inflation hit levels not seen in forty years. The gallon of milk, the tank of gas, the grocery bill: all of them lurched upward, and every parent in America felt it. The official explanation was "supply chain disruptions." The supply chains were disrupted. But trillions of newly created dollars chasing the same goods had something to do with the price increases too. That is not a controversial claim. It is arithmetic.

Here is where we are now.

The national debt of the United States is approaching thirty-nine trillion dollars. The interest on that debt exceeds one trillion dollars per year, more than the defense budget. The debt-to-GDP ratio is above one hundred and twenty percent, which means the country owes more than the total value of everything it produces in a year.

These numbers are not projections. They are not warnings. They are current.

And they are accelerating. The debt is growing by roughly seven and a half billion dollars per day. The interest payments are growing because the debt is growing, and the debt is growing partly because the interest payments are growing. This is a feedback loop. It has a name in mathematics: a compounding function. It has a name in common English too: a spiral.

The dollar, meanwhile, continues to lose purchasing power. Not dramatically, not overnight, not in a way that makes the evening news. Slowly. Persistently. In the price of eggs. In the price of rent. In the gap between what your paycheck says and what your paycheck buys. In the look on your face at the grocery checkout when the total comes up higher than it should.

That look is not confusion. It is the Cantillon effect, arriving at your kitchen table.

I want to connect this back to something from earlier in the book. In Chapter 3, I described the pattern: a civilization needs money, the money needs a ledger, the ledger starts honest, pressure builds, the ledger keeper adjusts the record, the money loses its meaning.

We are inside that pattern right now. The ledger keeper is the Federal Reserve. The adjustment is the expansion of the money supply. The meaning that is being lost is the purchasing power of the dollar—the thing your savings are denominated in, the thing your salary is paid in, the thing your children will inherit.

The pattern does not announce itself. Rome did not get a memo. Henry VIII did not hold a press conference. The Continentals did not come with a warning label. The pattern operates through prices, through purchasing power, through the slow erosion of what a unit of money actually means. Until one day it means something very different from what it meant when you started saving.

That day is not coming. It is here. It has been here since 1971. Most people have not noticed because the erosion is slow enough to explain away—year by year, price by price, grocery bill by grocery bill. But the numbers do not lie, even when the people quoting them do.

The next chapter is about what comes next: not next year, but next decade. The forces that are about to make this pressure worse, faster, in ways that most parents have not yet considered.

That is the chapter about artificial intelligence.

Chapter 7

The acceleration

In 2023, a friend of mine lost his job. He was a good copywriter, twenty years of experience, a client list that included Fortune 500 companies, a reputation for clean prose under deadline. He was not lazy. He was not expensive. He was replaced by a software program that could produce a first draft in eleven seconds.

He told me this at a birthday party, standing near the cooler, the way people deliver news they have not fully processed. He was not angry yet. He was confused. He had spent two decades getting good at something, and the something had become free overnight.

I tell this story not because it is unusual. I tell it because it is about to become ordinary.

This chapter is about artificial intelligence. Not the science fiction version: not the sentient machine, not the robot uprising, not the dystopia that makes a good movie trailer. The version that matters. The economic version. The version that is already here, already working, already changing the math on labor, wages, and government spending in ways that connect directly to everything this book has been building toward.

The connection is simple, and I want you to see it before we get into the details.

The pattern we have traced, government spends more than it collects, fills the gap by creating money, the money loses value, runs on pressure. The pressure comes from spending. And the single largest driver of government spending, in every developed nation on earth, is what happens when large numbers of people cannot find work.

Unemployment benefits. Retraining programs. Disability claims. Food assistance. Social Security drawn early. Healthcare for people who lost their employer coverage. The safety net, whatever you think of it politically, costs money. And when the number of people who need the net grows faster than the number of people paying into it, the gap gets filled the same way it has always been filled.

More money. Created faster. With the same consequences we have been tracing since Rome.

Artificial intelligence is about to make that gap very large, very fast.

I am a technologist. A parent and a consultant who has watched technology displace labor for twenty years. I watched dial-up replace the telegram. I watched email replace the fax. I watched the smartphone replace the Rolodex, the Thomas Guide, the camera store, the record store, the travel agent, the bank teller, and the taxi dispatcher. Each wave was faster than the one before. Each one eliminated jobs that the people holding them believed were permanent.

But every previous wave had a quality that made it survivable: it was narrow. The ATM replaced the bank teller but created jobs for ATM technicians. The spreadsheet replaced the bookkeeper but created jobs for analysts. The pattern was: technology automates a specific task, the humans who performed that task move to a different task, and the economy reorganizes.

What is different about artificial intelligence—and I want to be precise here, because imprecision on this topic breeds either panic or complacency, and neither one helps—is that it is not narrow. It is general.

A large language model does not automate one task. It automates the production of language itself, which means it touches every job that involves reading, writing, summarizing, analyzing, translating, coding, advising, explaining, or persuading. That is not a niche. That is most of the white-collar economy.

My copywriter friend was not replaced by a machine that writes copy. He was replaced by a machine that writes. The distinction matters. A machine that writes copy threatens copywriters. A machine that writes threatens anyone whose job is built on the written word.

I want to be careful not to overstate this. I have watched technology predictions go wrong too many times to traffic in certainty. The internet was supposed to eliminate retail, and retail is still here. E-books were supposed to eliminate print, and print is still here. The future arrives unevenly, and slower than the headlines suggest.

But the trend line is not ambiguous. The consulting firms, McKinsey, Goldman Sachs, the World

Economic Forum, are publishing reports with numbers that would have been science fiction five years ago. Estimates vary, but the range is striking: between three hundred million and eight hundred million jobs worldwide could be affected by AI within the next decade. Not eliminated overnight. Affected, which means transformed, reduced, restructured, or replaced.

Even the low end of that range represents the largest labor displacement in human history. Larger than the Industrial Revolution. Faster than anything that came before it.

Here is where this connects to money.

When people lose jobs, they need support. When they need support, the government spends. When the government spends more than it collects, it borrows. When it borrows more than it can repay through taxation, it creates money. When it creates money, the money already in circulation loses value. When the money loses value, the people who are already struggling, the ones who just lost their jobs, struggle more.

That is the spiral. We have seen it before. But the AI acceleration adds a variable that previous spirals did not have: speed.

The Industrial Revolution displaced millions of agricultural workers over the course of a century. They had time—painful, difficult, disruptive time, but time—to retrain, to move, to find new industries. The AI displacement is measured in quarters, not generations. A capability that did not exist in January exists in March. A job that was secure in April is automated by September. The economy does not reorganize that fast. Humans do not retrain that fast. And governments, faced with millions of displaced workers and a tax base that is shrinking precisely when spending needs to grow, will do what they have always done.

They will print money. Because printing money is the only response that does not require a vote, does not require a tax increase, does not require anyone to say the hard thing out loud. It is the quiet thing. The invisible thing. The thing that buys time until the next crisis.

And the next crisis will arrive faster than the last one, because the technology that is causing the displacement is itself accelerating.

I want to be clear about what I am not saying.

I am not saying AI is evil. I am not saying technology is the enemy. I am sitting in a room right now using tools that did not exist when my oldest child was born, and many of them make my life better. The question is not whether AI is good or bad. The question is: who pays the cost of the transition?

If the answer is "the people who hold dollars," and history says it will be, then every parent reading this book needs to understand that the dollars they are saving for their children's future are going to buy less of that future than they expect. Not because of a conspiracy. Not because of a villain. Because of a mechanism that is older than Rome and faster than anything Rome ever faced.

The pressure that took two hundred and fifty years to break Roman currency, that took four years to break Henry's coins, that has been compounding since 1913 and accelerating since 1971, that pressure is about to have a force multiplier.

The force multiplier is already here. It wrote a first draft in eleven seconds. And it is getting faster.

That is the end of Part Two. We have traced the line: money as technology, the ledger problem, the pattern of debasement, 1913, 1971, 2008, COVID, and the acceleration that is coming.

Part Three is the turn. It is about what can be done: specifically, about a technology that solves the ledger problem in a way that nobody solved it before. Not by trusting better people to keep the books. By building a system where nobody keeps the books. Where the books keep themselves.

If you have read this far, you are ready for it.

Part Three

Bitcoin, explained for a parent

Chapter 8

What Bitcoin is

On January 3, 2009, four months after Lehman Brothers collapsed, while the bailouts were still being counted, someone created the first block of a new monetary system. Embedded in that block, in the space normally reserved for technical data, was a line of text copied from the front page of The Times of London:

"Chancellor on brink of second bailout for banks."

Nobody knows who put it there. The creator used a pseudonym, Satoshi Nakamoto, and disappeared a few years later without ever revealing their identity. But the message was not subtle. It was a timestamp and a thesis, written into the foundation of a new technology, on the day the old one was being rescued from itself.

The technology was Bitcoin. And if you have read the first seven chapters of this book, you already understand most of what it is, because Bitcoin is the answer to a question we have been asking since Chapter 3.

Can you build a ledger that scales beyond a village but cannot be corrupted by the people who run it?

Remember Yap.

A limestone disc sits in front of a house. The whole village knows who owns it. When it changes hands, the whole village updates the record. Nobody writes it down. Nobody needs to. The community is the ledger. No single person—no chief, no priest, no banker—has the power to change the record. The memory is distributed across everyone.

That system had two virtues and one fatal limitation.

The virtues: the money was scarce (you could not fake a limestone disc quarried two hundred miles across open ocean) and the ledger was incorruptible (you could not change the memory of an entire village).

The limitation: it did not scale. It worked on an island of a few thousand people. It could not work in a city of a million, let alone a planet of eight billion. You cannot rely on everyone remembering everything. The village is too big.

Bitcoin is what happens when you solve the scaling problem without giving up the virtues.

I am going to explain Bitcoin the way I would explain it to a parent at a birthday party, which, as it happens, is exactly the context where I have explained it most often. No jargon. No code. No mathematics. Just the three properties from Chapter 1, scarcity, verification, and memory, and how Bitcoin satisfies each one.

Scarcity.

There will only ever be twenty-one million Bitcoin. Not approximately. Not "targeted at." Exactly twenty-one million. That number is written into the software that runs the network, and changing it would require convincing the majority of every computer running that software, tens of thousands of independent machines, in dozens of countries, operated by people who have every incentive to keep the limit exactly where it is.

This is not like a central bank promising to limit the money supply. This is not a policy that can be reversed at the next meeting. This is mathematics. The twenty-one million limit is enforced by the same mechanism that enforces the fact that two plus two equals four: it is built into the structure, and no committee can vote it away.

The Yap islanders' money was scarce because limestone was hard to quarry and oceans were hard to cross. Gold is scarce because physics made it rare in the earth's crust. Bitcoin is scarce because the code says so, and the code is run by thousands of independent operators who will not change it, because changing it would destroy the value of the Bitcoin they already hold.

The incentive and the structure point in the same direction. That is not an accident. It is the design.

Verification.

Every Bitcoin transaction that has ever occurred is recorded on a public ledger, a ledger that anyone can read, anyone can verify, and nobody can edit. If I send you one Bitcoin, that transaction is visible to every computer on the network. It is checked, confirmed, and written into the permanent record by machines that are designed to reject anything that does not follow the rules.

You do not need to trust me. You do not need to trust a bank. You do not need to trust a government. You can verify the transaction yourself, using free software, on a computer you control. The verification is not delegated to an authority. It is available to anyone who cares to look.

Gold could be tested: bitten, weighed, dropped in water. But testing gold required expertise, and storing gold required trusting someone with a vault. Bitcoin can be verified by anyone with an internet connection, and it can be stored without trusting anyone at all. We will come back to that in a later chapter.

Memory.

This is the big one. This is the property that makes Bitcoin different from everything that came before it.

Remember the problem. Every monetary system in history has required a ledger, a record of who owns what. And every ledger in history has been kept by someone: a village, a priest, a goldsmith, a bank, a government. Whoever keeps the ledger has the power to change it. And that power, given enough time and enough pressure, gets abused.

Bitcoin's ledger is not kept by anyone. It is kept by everyone.

Tens of thousands of computers around the world, in basements, in data centers, in warehouses, in apartments, each maintain a complete, identical copy of every transaction that has ever occurred on the network. When a new transaction happens, it is broadcast to all of them. They check it against the rules. If it is valid, they add it to their copy. If it is not valid, they reject it. No single computer has authority. No single operator has the power to change the record.

This is the Yap village, scaled to the planet. The memory is distributed. The record is public. And because everyone has a copy, nobody can cheat. Because cheating would mean changing your copy, and your copy would no longer match the thousands of other copies, and the network would reject your version. You cannot lie to a system where everyone is watching and everyone remembers.

There is a phrase for what secures Bitcoin's ledger, and you have heard it before in this book: proof of work.

The Yap islanders proved the value of their stones by crossing an ocean. Gold miners prove the value of gold by crushing rock. Bitcoin miners, and the word "miners" is used deliberately, prove the value of each new block of transactions by expending electricity. Enormous amounts of electricity. The computation is real. The energy is real. The cost is real.

This sounds wasteful until you understand what it is producing. It is not producing Bitcoin, exactly. It is producing security. The energy expenditure makes it astronomically expensive to forge a transaction or alter the historical record. To change a single entry in Bitcoin's ledger, you would need to outspend the combined computational power of the entire network, which is, at this point, larger than the computing capacity of any single government on earth.

The work is the wall. The wall protects the ledger. The ledger is the money.

A Yap stone carries proof of an ocean crossing. A gold coin carries proof of geological scarcity. A Bitcoin carries proof of computational work so expensive that forging it would cost more than stealing it honestly. The principle is the same. The scale is different.

I want to say something here about what this felt like the first time I understood it. Because I did not understand it at first. Most people do not.

When I first heard about Bitcoin, sometime around 2013, before I paid for my MIT course with it in 2017—my reaction was the same as most people's reaction. It sounded fake. It sounded like a scam, or a fad, or a toy for technologists. Internet money. Play money. Not real.

What changed my mind was not the technology. It was the history. Once I understood what had happened to the Roman denarius, what had happened to Henry's coins, what had happened to the Continental dollar, what had happened to the purchasing power of the dollar since 1913. Once I understood the pattern, I recognized Bitcoin for what it was. Not a new kind of money. A new kind of ledger.

The first ledger in history that cannot be edited by the people who run it.

That is all it is. Everything else—the price volatility, the exchange rate, the headlines, the hype, the crashes, the comebacks—is noise. The signal is the ledger. An incorruptible ledger, running on proof of work, with a fixed supply, maintained by thousands of independent operators who do not trust each other and do not need to.

The Yap islanders would have understood it immediately.

I know what you are thinking, because I have had this conversation a hundred times. You are thinking: but what about...?

What about the scams? What about the volatility? What about the criminals who use it? What about the energy? What about the government banning it?

Those are real questions. They deserve honest answers, not dismissals. The next chapter is nothing but those questions, asked directly and answered directly. Because if this book asks you to take Bitcoin seriously, it owes you the courtesy of taking your objections seriously first.

Chapter 9

What Bitcoin isn't

Every time I mention Bitcoin in conversation, at a dinner, at a school event, at the edge of a birthday party where the parents have drifted toward the serious end of the yard, I get the same look. It is the look of someone who has heard the word before and has already decided what it means.

It means scam. Or gambling. Or that thing my brother-in-law lost money on. Or dark web. Or Elon Musk. Or that guy who threw away a hard drive with seventy million dollars on it.

I have learned not to argue with the look. I ask instead. What specifically concerns you? And the concerns, when they come out, are almost always the same five or six questions, asked in slightly different words by slightly different people. They are reasonable questions. They deserve real answers.

This chapter is nothing but those answers.

"It's a scam."

This is the most common objection and the easiest to understand. People have been burned. Not by Bitcoin, but by things that called themselves Bitcoin, or crypto, or blockchain, or Web3. The landscape around Bitcoin is littered with fraud. FTX. Luna. Bitconnect. Ponzi schemes dressed in whitepapers. Celebrities hawking tokens they did not understand. Exchanges that collapsed because the people running them were stealing the deposits.

All of that is real. None of it is Bitcoin.

This is the distinction that matters, and it is the one that almost everyone misses: Bitcoin is not "crypto." Bitcoin is a specific technology with a specific design, running on a specific network that has operated continuously since January 2009 without a single minute of downtime. It has no CEO. It has no marketing department. It has no venture capital investors. Nobody can change the rules because nobody is in charge of the rules.

The scams happen in the ecosystem around Bitcoin, in the exchanges, the altcoins, the tokens, the influencers. That ecosystem is exactly as trustworthy as any unregulated market full of money and human nature. Which is to say: not very.

But confusing Bitcoin with the scams built around it is like confusing gold with the people who sell fake gold watches on Canal Street. The watches are fake. The gold is not.

“It’s too volatile.”

This one is fair, on the surface. Bitcoin’s price, measured in dollars, moves dramatically. It has dropped fifty percent or more on several occasions. It has also risen thousands of percent over the past fifteen years. The short-term movements are violent enough to make any reasonable person nervous.

But the objection contains a hidden assumption: that the dollar is the stable thing and Bitcoin is the unstable thing. That assumption is worth examining.

The dollar loses purchasing power every year. It has lost more than ninety-five percent since 1913. That loss is slow, persistent, and compounding, like a leak in a roof that never gets fixed. You do not notice the leak on any given day. You notice it when the ceiling falls in.

Bitcoin's volatility is the opposite: dramatic in the short term, upward over the long term. A parent who bought one hundred dollars of Bitcoin in any year prior to 2020 and simply held it has more purchasing power today than when they started. That is not true of the dollar over any comparable period.

I am not saying Bitcoin is not volatile. It is. I am saying that "volatile" is not the same as "risky," and "stable" is not the same as "safe." A dollar that loses three percent of its value every year, predictably, for fifty years, is not safe. It is a slow-motion loss dressed in the language of stability.

Volatility is the price of a young technology being priced by the market in real time. Debasement is the price of an old technology being managed by people with no reason to stop.

Pick your risk.

"Criminals use it."

Yes. Criminals also use the dollar. In enormously greater volume.

The United Nations estimates that between two and five percent of global GDP, roughly two trillion dollars per year, is laundered through the traditional banking system. Drug cartels. Arms dealers. Human traffickers. Sanctions evaders. They use dollars. They use euros. They use the global banking system, which has been fined hundreds of billions of dollars over the past two decades for facilitating exactly this kind of activity. HSBC. Deutsche Bank. Wachovia. The fines are large. The behavior continues.

Bitcoin is actually worse for criminals than cash, because every transaction is recorded on a public ledger that anyone can read. Cash leaves no trail. Bitcoin leaves a permanent one. Law enforcement has figured this out. The FBI, the IRS, Europol all use blockchain analysis to trace criminal transactions, and they are getting better at it every year. The Colonial Pipeline ransom was recovered because the Bitcoin could be tracked. Try tracking a suitcase of hundred-dollar bills.

The "criminals use it" argument is not wrong. It is incomplete. Criminals use every form of money. The relevant question is: does this form of money make crime easier or harder to trace? Bitcoin makes it harder to hide. Cash makes it trivial.

"It wastes energy."

Bitcoin mining uses a lot of electricity. That is true and worth taking seriously. The network consumes roughly as much energy as a small country, comparable to Argentina or Norway, depending on the year and the estimate.

The question is: compared to what?

The traditional financial system, the banks, the data centers, the ATM networks, the armored trucks, the office towers, the trading floors, the compliance departments, consumes far more energy than Bitcoin. It also employs millions of people whose jobs exist primarily to manage the complexity of a centralized trust system. Bitcoin replaces that complexity with mathematics. The energy is the cost of that replacement.

But there is a more important point. Bitcoin miners consume electricity, and electricity has a cost. They will only mine if the revenue exceeds the cost. This creates a relentless incentive to find the cheapest energy available, which, increasingly, is renewable energy and stranded energy that would otherwise be wasted. Flared natural gas at oil wells. Excess hydroelectric power in rainy seasons. Geothermal energy in Iceland. Bitcoin miners are, economically, the buyers of last resort for energy that nobody else wants.

That does not make the energy consumption zero. It does make the narrative, that Bitcoin is boiling the planet, considerably more complicated than the headlines suggest.

"The government will ban it."

Some have tried. China banned Bitcoin mining in 2021. Miners publicly relocated to Texas, Kazakhstan, anywhere the electricity was cheap and the government was welcoming. The network dipped for a few weeks and recovered. Here is the part worth knowing: despite the ban, China remains one of the largest Bitcoin mining locations on the planet. The miners did not all leave. They went underground. An authoritarian government with the most sophisticated surveillance apparatus on earth could not stop its own citizens from running the software. That is not a talking point. That is a stress test.

Bitcoin does not run on a server that can be seized. It does not operate through a company that can be shut down. It runs on tens of thousands of independent computers in dozens of countries. Banning Bitcoin in one jurisdiction is like banning email in one country. The technology does not care about borders.

Could the United States ban it? In theory. In practice, the US has moved in the opposite direction, toward regulation, not prohibition. Bitcoin ETFs now trade on major exchanges. Banks are building custody services. The political incentive has shifted from "this is dangerous" to "we should not be the country that drives this technology offshore."

But even in the worst case, a total ban everywhere, the network would continue to run. It was designed to survive exactly that scenario. The people who built it had read the same history this book is built on. They knew what governments do to money they cannot control. They built accordingly.

"I missed it. It's too expensive."

A Bitcoin costs tens of thousands of dollars. That sounds like a barrier until you learn that you do not have to buy a whole one.

Bitcoin is divisible to eight decimal places. The smallest unit, one hundred millionth of a Bitcoin, is called a satoshi. You can buy ten dollars of Bitcoin. You can buy fifty. You can buy whatever amount fits your budget, the same way you can buy a gram of gold without buying a whole bar.

The question is not whether you can afford a Bitcoin. The question is whether the dollars you are not converting into Bitcoin are going to hold their value over the next twenty years. If you have read the preceding chapters, you already know my answer to that question.

But I am not going to tell you what to do with your money. That is not what this book is for. The next chapter, on self-custody, is about what happens after you decide. For now, the only thing I want you to take away is this: the objections are real, they are worth asking, and they do not change the fundamental design.

Bitcoin is scarce. The ledger is public. The record is incorruptible. No single person or institution controls it.

Everything else is a question about adoption, regulation, and human behavior, the same questions that surrounded every important technology ever built. The telephone was a toy. The automobile was dangerous. The internet was for criminals.

The technology survived the objections. Every time.

Chapter 10

Self-custody

There is a phrase in Bitcoin that sounds like a bumper sticker but functions like a law of physics: not your keys, not your coins.

It means: if you do not hold the keys to your Bitcoin yourself, you do not own your Bitcoin. You own a promise from whoever does hold the keys. And if this book has taught you anything, it is that promises about money, given enough time and enough pressure, get broken.

This chapter is about what self-custody is, why it matters, and why it is the single most important concept a parent can understand before putting a single dollar into Bitcoin.

Start with what a "key" actually is, because the word is doing real work here.

When you own Bitcoin, what you actually own is a string of characters, a private key, that gives you the ability to move your Bitcoin on the ledger. Think of it as a password, except this password has no "forgot my password" link. There is no customer service number. There is no company that can reset it. The key is yours. If you have it, you control your Bitcoin. If you lose it, nobody can help you.

That sounds terrifying. It is supposed to. Because the alternative, the thing most people do instead, is to hand their keys to someone else and trust that person to hold them honestly.

The "someone else" is usually an exchange. Coinbase. Kraken. Binance. You open an account, deposit dollars, buy Bitcoin, and the exchange holds the Bitcoin for you. Your account shows a balance. The balance feels real. It feels like a bank account.

It is not a bank account. Your bank account is insured by the FDIC up to $250,000. If the bank fails, the government guarantees your deposit. No such guarantee exists for a Bitcoin exchange. If the exchange fails, your Bitcoin is gone. If the exchange is hacked, your Bitcoin is gone. If the person running the exchange turns out to be a fraud, your Bitcoin is gone.

This is not hypothetical. FTX was the second-largest cryptocurrency exchange in the world. It held billions of dollars in customer deposits. In November 2022, it collapsed in less than a week. The founder was convicted of fraud. The customer funds were missing. Billions of dollars, belonging to millions of people who thought they owned crypto. They did not own crypto. They owned a line item on someone else's spreadsheet.

Not your keys, not your coins.

Self-custody means you hold the keys yourself. You do not trust an exchange. You do not trust a bank. You do not trust a company. You take possession of the thing, the way your grandmother took possession of her cash when she put it in envelopes in the kitchen drawer.

The tools for self-custody are simple. A hardware wallet is a small device, roughly the size of a USB drive, that stores your private keys offline. It is not connected to the internet. It cannot be hacked remotely. When you want to send Bitcoin, you plug the device in, confirm the transaction on the device's screen, and unplug it. The keys never leave the device.

The most popular hardware wallets cost between fifty and two hundred dollars. They are not complicated to use. They are less complicated than setting up a new smartphone. If you can follow the instructions that come in the box, you can custody your own Bitcoin.

There is also a backup: a set of twelve or twenty-four words, called a seed phrase, that can regenerate your keys if the device is lost or destroyed. Write the words down. On paper. Store the paper somewhere safe. A fireproof safe. A safety deposit box. Your parents' house. Do not store the words on a computer. Do not take a photo of them. Do not email them to yourself. Paper, pen, safe place. That is the backup.

I can hear the objection forming. It sounds like this: "That is insane. You want me to be my own bank? What if I lose the words? What if there is a fire? What if I die and my family cannot access it?"

These are not objections. These are engineering problems. And they have solutions.

The seed phrase can be stamped into steel, which survives fire and flood. Companies sell steel plates designed for exactly this purpose, for about thirty dollars. Your seed phrase, engraved in metal, stored in a safe. That is more durable than any bank vault and considerably less expensive.

For the question of death or incapacity, the solution is the same as for any other asset: estate planning. You write down what your heirs need to know and where to find it, and you store that information the same way you store your will. A sealed envelope with a trusted attorney. A letter in a safe with instructions. This is not different from what you already do with life insurance policies and account passwords. It is one more item on the list.

Multi-signature setups add another layer. Instead of a single key, you can require two out of three keys to move your Bitcoin. One key with you. One with your spouse. One with a trusted family member or an attorney. No single person can move the funds. No single key being lost or stolen compromises the whole. This is the tally stick principle from Chapter 3, applied to digital money. Split the control. Distribute the trust.

Here is why this matters enough to deserve its own chapter.

The entire argument of this book rests on one idea: whoever controls the ledger controls the money. Rome controlled the ledger and debased the coins.

Henry controlled the ledger and debased the coins. The Federal Reserve controls the ledger and has expanded the money supply by a factor of a thousand since 1913.

Bitcoin solved the ledger problem. Nobody controls Bitcoin's ledger. But if you store your Bitcoin on an exchange, you have reintroduced the problem at the last mile. You have taken money that exists on an incorruptible ledger and placed it under the control of a corruptible institution. You have rebuilt the single point of failure that Bitcoin was designed to eliminate.

Self-custody is not a technical preference. It is the entire point.

When you hold your own keys, your Bitcoin cannot be frozen by a bank. It cannot be seized by an exchange that is going bankrupt. It cannot be inflated by a central authority. It cannot be confiscated without physical access to your device or your seed phrase. It is yours in a way that no other financial asset in the modern world is yours.

Your bank account is yours until the bank fails, or the government freezes it, or a court orders it seized. Your brokerage account is yours until the broker fails, or the regulator suspends trading, or the counterparty defaults. These are not paranoid fantasies. They are documented events. They happened in Cyprus in 2013, when the government seized a percentage of bank deposits to fund a bailout. They happened in Canada in 2022, when the government froze the bank accounts of political protesters.

Self-custody removes the counterparty. There is nobody between you and your money. That is the point.

I want to end this chapter with something practical, because this book is written for parents, and parents do not have time for theory that does not land somewhere useful.

If you decide to own Bitcoin, and that is your decision to make, not mine, here is the minimum you need to know about holding it:

Buy a hardware wallet from a reputable manufacturer. Coldcard, Trezor, and Ledger are the names most often recommended. Buy it directly from the manufacturer, not from a third party.

Set it up following the manufacturer's instructions. Write down the seed phrase on paper. Do not skip this step. Do not store it digitally.

Transfer your Bitcoin from the exchange to your hardware wallet. The exchange will have instructions for withdrawal. It takes a few minutes.

Store the seed phrase in a secure location separate from the device. If the device is in your home office, the seed phrase should be in a safe, or at a relative's house, or with an attorney.

Tell one trusted person where the seed phrase is and what it is for. Not the words themselves. The location. In case something happens to you.

That is it. The entire process takes less than an hour. The result is that you hold your own money, on your own terms, without depending on any institution to keep its promise.

Your grandmother's envelopes in the kitchen drawer, updated for the twenty-first century.

Chapter 11

What you should actually do

I am not a financial advisor. I am not going to pretend to be one. This chapter does not contain investment advice, and if anyone tells you it does, hand them this paragraph and walk away.

What this chapter contains is the framework I use for my own family. Four children. Twenty years of watching markets from the inside. A clinical social work background that taught me people do not make good decisions when they are scared, and a consulting career that taught me they do not make good decisions when they are rushed. The best decisions come from understanding the situation clearly and acting from a position of calm.

Here is the situation, clearly.

The dollar is losing purchasing power. It has been losing purchasing power for over a century. The rate of loss is accelerating. The forces driving the acceleration, government debt, monetary expansion, AI-driven labor displacement, are structural, not temporary. No elected official in either party has proposed a credible plan to reverse them, because reversing them would require saying things that cost elections.

Your savings, your retirement account, your children's college fund: all of them are denominated in dollars. All of them are subject to this erosion. The question is not whether the erosion will continue. The question is what, if anything, you want to do about it.

The first thing to do is nothing dramatic.

I mean this seriously. The worst financial decisions are made in a state of urgency. If you have read this book and feel a rising alarm, that alarm is understandable, but it is not a plan. Do not sell everything and buy Bitcoin tomorrow. Do not empty your 401(k). Do not do anything that would put your family in a difficult position if Bitcoin dropped fifty percent next month, because it might. It has before. It probably will again.

The right posture is not panic. It is preparation.

Here is what preparation looks like, in practical terms.

Start by understanding what you already have. Most families have their wealth in three or four places: a bank account, a retirement account, a house, and maybe some savings bonds or a brokerage account. All of these are denominated in dollars. All of them are subject to the same erosion we have been discussing.

The house is different from the others. Real estate tends to hold value during inflationary periods, because the price of the house rises roughly with the price of everything else. You are not losing purchasing power on your house the way you are losing it on your cash savings. The house is a real asset. Keep it.

The retirement account is more complicated. The money in your 401(k) or IRA is invested in stocks, bonds, or a mix of both. Stocks, over long periods, tend to outpace inflation. Bonds do not. If your retirement account is heavily weighted toward bonds, you are holding a promise to be paid a fixed number of future dollars, and those future dollars will buy less than today's dollars. That is worth understanding. Talk to whoever manages your account. Ask them what happens to your portfolio if inflation runs at five or six percent for the next decade. Watch their face.

The bank account is the most vulnerable. Cash sitting in a savings account earning two or three percent interest while inflation runs at four or five percent is losing value every day. It feels safe. It is not safe. It is the slow-motion loss we discussed in Chapter 9.

Here is where Bitcoin fits. Not as a replacement for everything you own. As one piece of a broader approach.

The concept is simple: take a small percentage of your savings, an amount you could afford to lose entirely without it changing your life, and convert it to Bitcoin. Hold it in self-custody, on a hardware wallet, using the process described in the last chapter. Then do nothing. Do not trade it. Do not watch the price every day. Do not sell it when it drops. Do not buy more when it spikes. Set it and leave it.

How much? That is your decision. Some people start with one percent of their savings. Some start with five. Some, after studying the subject for years, hold much more. I am not going to tell you a number. I am going to tell you a principle: the right amount is the amount that lets you sleep at night, in both directions. You should not lose sleep worrying about the Bitcoin. You should not lose sleep worrying about the dollars either.

The strategy has a name in investing. It is called asymmetric risk. You risk a small amount. The downside is limited: you can lose what you put in. The upside is not limited in the same way: if Bitcoin continues the trajectory it has followed for fifteen years, a small allocation today could become a meaningful portion of your family's wealth in a decade.

That is not a guarantee. Nothing in investing is a guarantee. But the asymmetry is real, and it is worth understanding.

There is a second strategy, and it is even simpler: dollar-cost averaging.

Instead of buying a lump sum, you buy a fixed dollar amount of Bitcoin at regular intervals. Fifty dollars a month. A hundred dollars a month. Whatever fits your budget. You buy when the price is high. You buy when the price is low. Over time, the purchases average out, and you accumulate Bitcoin without trying to time the market.

Timing the market does not work. It does not work with stocks. It does not work with real estate. It does not work with Bitcoin. The people who try to buy low and sell high almost always buy high and sell low, because human psychology is wired for exactly the wrong behavior. We buy when we are excited, which is when prices are high. We sell when we are scared, which is when prices are low.

Dollar-cost averaging removes the psychology. It replaces emotion with arithmetic. Set up an automatic purchase, the same way you set up automatic transfers to a savings account, and let time do the work.

A note about your children.

If you have a child who is old enough to receive an allowance, they are old enough to learn about saving in Bitcoin. I am not suggesting you hand a seven-year-old a hardware wallet. I am suggesting you set aside a small amount of Bitcoin in their name, on a wallet you control, and tell them about it.

The conversation does not need to be complicated. "This is money that nobody can print more of. It sits on a ledger that nobody can change. When you are older, I will show you how to hold it yourself." That is enough. The concept will grow with them.

For older children, teenagers, the conversation can go deeper. Show them the purchasing power chart of the dollar since 1913. Let them do the math on what a dollar bought when their grandparents were young. Ask them what they think will happen to the dollars in their savings account over the next fifty years. Do not lecture. Ask. Let them arrive at the conclusion themselves.

This is the hardest part of this chapter to write, because it is the part where the book becomes personal. I did this with my own children. I started the conversation years ago, before I started writing books about it. The conversations were awkward at first. They got better. My children understand something that most adults do not: the money they earn is losing value while it sits in their pocket, and there is an alternative.

That understanding is worth more than the Bitcoin itself.

Here is what I am not telling you to do.

I am not telling you to go all in. I am not telling you to take on debt to buy Bitcoin. I am not telling you to sell your house. I am not telling you to cash out your retirement account. Anyone who tells you to do any of those things is not looking out for your family.

I am telling you to learn. To understand the system your money operates in. To understand why that system is structured the way it is, who benefits from the structure, and what the alternatives are. And then to make a decision, calmly, based on what you know, not what you feel.

The goal is not to get rich. The goal is to not get poor slowly, invisibly, in a way you never saw coming because nobody told you it was happening.

Now someone has told you.

The rest is up to you. But before you close this book, there is one more section. It is about the conversation itself: how to talk to your children about money, what to say, what to listen for, and how a story about a village called Stonewater might be the best way to start.

Part Four

Having the conversation

Chapter 12

How to talk to a child about money

The conversation you are about to have with your child is not a lecture. If it turns into a lecture, you have lost them. Children do not learn from lectures. They learn from stories, from questions, and from watching what you do when you think they are not paying attention.

They are always paying attention.

I learned this the hard way. My first attempt to explain money to my oldest was a disaster. I sat down at the kitchen table with a serious look on my face and started talking about inflation, purchasing power, and the Federal Reserve. I might as well have been reading from a textbook. Her eyes went glassy inside thirty seconds. She asked if she could go play. I said yes. I sat at the table for a while after that, thinking about what I had done wrong.

What I had done wrong was start with the answer. Children do not care about answers to questions they have not asked. The trick, and it took me years to learn it, is to start with the question. Not your question. Theirs.

Every child, at some point, asks a version of the same question. It shows up differently at different ages, but the core is always the same: why can't we just have more money?

A five-year-old says it directly: "Why can't you just get more money?" A ten-year-old frames it as fairness: "Why does everything cost so much?" A teenager frames it as frustration: "How am I supposed to afford college when you could buy a house for what I am paying for a semester?"

Each of these is an invitation. Not to explain the Federal Reserve. To explore.

Here is what works, broken down by the age ranges I have tested it on with my own children and in conversations with other parents over the years.

Ages five to seven. At this age, children understand trading. They trade snacks at the lunch table. They trade toys in the backyard. They understand, instinctively, that some things are harder to get than others, and that the hard-to-get things are worth more.

Start there. Ask them: if everyone could find gold in their backyard, would gold be special? They will say no. Ask them why. They will say because everyone would have it. Congratulations. You have just taught scarcity to a six-year-old without using the word.

Then ask: what if you found something really rare, but nobody else wanted it? Would it be valuable? They will think about it. They will probably say no. You have just taught them the difference between scarcity and value. That distinction trips up adults. Your six-year-old got it in two questions.

Do not push further than this in a single conversation. One concept per sitting. Let it marinate. They will come back with questions of their own, and those questions will be better than anything you could have planned.

Ages eight to eleven. This is the sweet spot. Children at this age can handle longer stories. They understand unfairness. They are beginning to notice that the world does not work the way they were told it works.

This is the age to introduce the idea that money is not a thing, it is a technology. Use the examples from this book. Tell them about the Yap stones. Tell them about salt caravans in Ethiopia. Tell them about the tally sticks that burned down Parliament. Kids love that one. It has fire.

Ask them: if you and your friend both kept a list of who owed whom cookies, and your lists disagreed, who would be right? They will argue about it. Let them. They are discovering the ledger problem. They are discovering it the same way the Yap islanders discovered it, and the goldsmiths of London, and the architects of Bitcoin. The question is always the same: who keeps the books?

At this age, you can also start the allowance experiment. Give them their allowance in two forms: some in dollars, some in Bitcoin (held on a wallet you control, shown to them as a number). Let them watch both over time. The dollars will sit flat. The Bitcoin will move. Sometimes up. Sometimes down. Over a year, the comparison will teach them more about monetary systems than any book, including this one.

Ages twelve and up. Teenagers can handle the full argument. They can understand inflation. They can understand debt. They can read a chart. And they are angry enough about the world to want an explanation for why things feel harder than they should.

Show them the dollar purchasing power chart. It is one image: a line that starts at the top left in 1913 and drops to the bottom right today. Let them stare at it. Ask them what they think it means. Do not tell them. Ask.

Then tell them about the diploma. Your father's diploma, MIT, 1947, four hundred dollars. Show them what MIT costs today. Let them do the division. The buildings are the same buildings. Let them sit with that.

Teenagers respond to being treated as equals in the conversation. They do not respond to being told what to think. If you present the facts and ask genuine questions, not rhetorical questions designed to lead them to your conclusion, but actual questions you are curious to hear them answer, they will engage. If you lecture, they will tune out. This is true of teenagers in general. It is especially true of a topic this loaded.

A few principles that apply across all ages.

Do not make it about politics. The moment you say "the government is stealing from us" or "both parties are corrupt," you have turned a conversation about money into a conversation about teams, and children (like adults) will pick a team and stop listening. Stick to the mechanics. The dollar buys less than it used to. Here is why. Here is what you can do about it.

Do not make it about fear. Children absorb their parents' anxiety with terrifying efficiency. If you are panicked about the economy, they will be panicked about the economy, and panic does not produce learning. It produces nightmares. Be calm. Be factual. Treat the subject the way you would treat a conversation about nutrition or exercise: this is how the world works, here is what we do about it, and we are going to be fine because we understand it.

Do not pretend to have all the answers. Children respect honesty more than expertise. If your child asks you something you do not know, say so. "I don't know. Let's find out together." That sentence is more powerful than any explanation in this book, because it models the behavior you want them to carry through their entire financial life: curiosity, humility, and the willingness to learn.

Start the conversation. That is the most important thing. It does not have to be perfect. It does not have to be complete. It just has to happen. Because if you do not have this conversation with your children, the world will have it for them, and the world's version will not include the parts that matter.

If you have a copy of Mara and the Stones of Stonewater, the next chapter is a guide to reading it with your child in a way that brings all of these concepts to life through story. If you do not have a copy, skip to Chapter 14, where I answer the questions your children are most likely to ask.

Chapter 13

Reading Mara with your child

I wrote Mara and the Stones of Stonewater before I wrote this book. It was designed to do something specific: to plant the concepts of sound money in a child's imagination before anyone tells them what to think about money. Story first, framework later. The same principle that governs this book governs that one.

If you do not have a copy, skip to Chapter 14. Everything in this book stands on its own. But if you do have a copy, or if you decide to get one, this chapter is a guide to reading it with your child in a way that turns a bedtime story into the beginning of a financial education.

You do not need to explain any of this to your child while you read. The story does the work. Your job is to ask the right questions afterward and listen carefully to the answers.

Mara is a girl who lives in a village called Stonewater. The village uses stones as money. The stones come from a place called the Deep Quarry, far from the village, difficult and dangerous to reach. There are forty-one stones. The whole village remembers who owns which stone. And every villager knows a recitation, passed down through generations, that encodes the rules of their monetary system in four lines a child can memorize.

That is the setup. Here is what each element is really about, and what to listen for when your child encounters it.

The Deep Quarry.

The stones of Stonewater are not picked up off the ground. They come from a quarry that requires real effort, real time, and real risk to reach. The journey is hard. That is not an accident in the story. The difficulty of obtaining a stone is what gives the stone its value.

This is proof of work. The same concept that makes gold valuable (it is hard to mine), that made the Yap stones valuable (it was dangerous to transport them), and that secures the Bitcoin network (it is expensive to produce each block).

After reading, ask your child: "Why do you think the stones come from somewhere far away? What would happen if the villagers could just pick up stones from the riverbank?"

Your child will likely say the stones would not be special anymore. That is the right answer. They have just understood scarcity and proof of work in the time it takes to answer one question. Let the answer sit. Do not explain further unless they ask.

The forty-one stones.

There is a fixed number of stones in Stonewater. Not "approximately forty-one." Not "about forty-one." Forty-one. The number does not change. New stones are not created. Old stones are not destroyed.

This is a fixed monetary supply. It is what gold approximates (the total amount of gold on earth is finite, though slowly increasing) and what Bitcoin achieves exactly (twenty-one million, forever).

Ask your child: "What would happen if someone figured out how to make new stones?" Listen to what they say. Some children will say the stones would be worth less. Some will say it would be unfair. Some will say the village would be angry. All of these are correct, and each one opens a different conversation.

If your child says the stones would be worth less, they are thinking about inflation. If they say it would be unfair, they are thinking about the Cantillon effect, though they will never use that phrase. If they say the village would be angry, they are thinking about trust and social contracts. Follow whichever thread they pull.

The community memory.

In Stonewater, there is no bank. There is no vault. There is no single person who keeps the records. The entire village remembers who owns which stone. When a stone changes hands, the village knows. The memory is shared.

This is a distributed ledger. It is the Yap system. It is, conceptually, the Bitcoin blockchain: a record maintained by everyone, controlled by no one.

Ask your child: “What if one person in the village tried to say they owned a stone that was not theirs? What would happen?” Your child will say the village would know they were lying. Press gently: “How would they know?" Because everyone remembers. Because the record is not kept in one place. Because you cannot fool a whole village.

Your child has just described the security model of Bitcoin. They described it in thirty seconds, and they did not need to know what a hash function is.

The recitation.

At the heart of the story is a recitation that the villagers know by heart:

A stone is worth the journey that it took. A stone is known by every eye that looked. No one can take what everyone remembers. The ledger lives in us like light in embers.

Each line corresponds to one of the principles this book has spent thirteen chapters building.

The first line is proof of work. The stone's value comes from the cost of obtaining it. The journey is the proof.

The second line is verification. The stone is known, visible, checked by every person who sees it. It cannot be counterfeited because everyone has seen the real one.

The third line is the security of distributed memory. You cannot steal what the whole community remembers. No single thief, no single authority, can alter a record that lives in everyone.

The fourth line is the beauty of the thing. The ledger is alive. It is not a spreadsheet in a vault. It is a living memory, carried by people, glowing like embers that do not go out.

Do not explain the recitation to your child. Let them hear it. Let them memorize it, if they want to. The words will do their work over years, the way all good poetry does. Your child does not need to know that the recitation is about monetary theory. They need to know the words. The understanding comes later, and it comes deeper because the words were there first.

How to read the book together.

Read it straight through the first time. Do not stop to explain. Do not pause to draw parallels. Just read it as a story. Let your child enjoy the village, the characters, the tension, the resolution. Stories work because they are experienced, not analyzed.

The second time through, slow down. Ask the questions I have suggested above. One or two per sitting. Do not turn it into a quiz. A quiz kills the magic. A conversation preserves it.

If your child asks a question you cannot answer, say so. Then look it up together. Some of the best conversations I have had with my children about money started with "I don't know, let's figure it out."

If your child is not interested, do not force it. Put the book on the shelf. It will still be there when they are ready. Every child arrives at these questions on their own timeline. The book is patient.

A note on what your child will teach you.

I have watched children read this story. I have listened to what they say afterward. And the thing that surprises me every time is how quickly they grasp what adults struggle with.

Adults have been trained to think of money as a thing. Children have not been trained yet. When you tell a child that the stones of Stonewater are valuable because of the journey it took to get them, the child does not argue. It makes sense to them. Effort equals value. They know this from the playground.

When you tell a child that the whole village remembers who owns which stone, the child does not find this strange. Of course they do. That is how fairness works. Everyone knows. Nobody can cheat.

When you tell an adult the same things, the adult pushes back. “But that is not how money works.” “But the government backs the dollar.” “But you need banks.” The adult has been living inside the system so long that the system feels like nature. The child has not. The child sees the system for what it is: a set of choices. Some good. Some not.

Listen to your child. They may understand this better than you expect.

Chapter 14

Questions your children will ask

Children ask better questions than adults. Adults ask questions they already know the answer to, looking for confirmation. Children ask questions they actually want answered. That makes them harder to prepare for and more important to get right.

Here are the questions I have been asked most often, by my own children and by other people's children, once the conversation about money gets started. I have included the answers I give. They are not the only answers. They are honest ones.

"What is money?"

Money is a tool that lets people trade with each other without having to swap the exact things they need. If you raise chickens and you need shoes, money lets you sell the chickens to one person and buy shoes from another. Without money, you would have to find a shoemaker who happens to want chickens. That is hard. Money makes it easy.

But here is the important part: not all money is the same. Some money holds its value over time. Some money loses its value. The difference matters, and most grown-ups never learned it.

"Why can't we just print more money?"

We can. We do. That is the problem.

When someone prints more money, the money that already exists becomes worth less. Imagine you and your friends are playing a game, and there are ten tokens, and each token buys one piece of candy. Now someone dumps a hundred more tokens into the game. There are a hundred and ten tokens, but there is still the same amount of candy. Each token buys a lot less candy than it did before.

That is what happens when the government prints money. The number of dollars goes up, but the amount of stuff stays roughly the same. So everything costs more. That is called inflation.

"Why does everything cost so much more than it used to?"

Because the money has gotten weaker. Not because the things got more expensive. Your great-grandparents could buy a house for a few thousand dollars. That was not because houses were cheap. It was because dollars were strong.

Since 1913, the dollar has lost more than ninety-five percent of its strength. So a thing that cost one dollar in 1913 costs more than twenty dollars today. The thing did not change. The dollar did.

"Is Bitcoin real money?"

That depends on what you mean by real. You cannot hold a Bitcoin in your hand. But you cannot hold most dollars in your hand either. Most dollars are numbers on a screen in a bank's computer. The dollars in your parents' bank account are not sitting in a vault somewhere. They are entries in a database.

Bitcoin is also entries in a database. The difference is: no single person controls Bitcoin's database. It is run by thousands of computers all over the world, and nobody can change the records. With regular money, the people in charge can create more of it whenever they want. With Bitcoin, they cannot. There will only ever be twenty-one million. That is written into the rules, and nobody can change the rules.

So yes. It is real. It is as real as any money that has ever existed. It is just built differently.

"Can someone steal my Bitcoin?"

Not if you hold it correctly. If you keep your Bitcoin on your own device, with your own keys, the only way someone can take it is if they physically get your keys. Nobody can hack it from across the internet. Nobody can freeze your account. Nobody at a company can lose it.

If you give your Bitcoin to someone else to hold for you, like a website or an app, then yes, that person could lose it or steal it. That has happened. That is why we keep our own keys. Not your keys, not your coins.

"Why don't they teach this in school?"

That is a very good question. The short answer is: most teachers were never taught it themselves. The things you are learning right now about money, about how it works and why it loses value, these are not part of most school curricula. Not because they are secret. Because the system that runs the schools is the same system that runs the money, and that system does not have a strong incentive to explain its own mechanics.

That is not a conspiracy. It is just how systems work. The people inside a system rarely explain the system to the people the system serves. That is why your parents are having this conversation with you instead of your teacher.

"Is the dollar going to become worthless?"

I do not know. Nobody does. What I can tell you is that the dollar has lost most of its value over the past hundred years, and the forces that caused that loss are still operating. They are actually getting stronger.

Will the dollar go to zero? Probably not in your lifetime. But it does not have to go to zero to hurt you. A dollar that loses three or four percent of its value every year, quietly, for thirty years, has lost more than half its purchasing power by the time you notice. That is not a crash. That is a slow fade. It is harder to see, which makes it harder to prepare for.

That is why we are having this conversation. So you can see it.

"Should I buy Bitcoin?"

When you are old enough to earn your own money and make your own decisions, that will be up to you. Right now, your parents are setting some aside for you, and when you are ready, we will teach you how to hold it yourself.

What I want you to understand right now is not "buy Bitcoin." It is: the money in your pocket is changing. It has been changing for a long time. Most people do not know that, and the ones who do not know it will lose purchasing power without understanding why. You know. That puts you ahead of almost everyone.

What you do with that knowledge is your call. But you will make a better decision because you have it.

"What if Bitcoin fails?"

It might. Any technology can fail. The internet could have failed. Electricity could have remained a curiosity. The printing press could have been suppressed.

But Bitcoin has been running since 2009 without stopping. It has survived government bans, exchange collapses, price crashes of more than eighty percent, and every form of attack that governments, hackers, and skeptics have been able to throw at it. It is still running. The ledger is still intact. The twenty-one million limit has not changed.

That does not mean it cannot fail. It means that everything that was supposed to kill it so far has not. And the longer it runs, the harder it becomes to stop, because the network gets bigger, the security gets stronger, and the number of people who depend on it grows.

Could it fail? Yes. Has it? Not yet. And "not yet," after seventeen years of continuous operation, starts to mean something.

"Why do you care about this so much?"

Because I am your parent, and it is my job to prepare you for the world you are actually going to live in, not the world I grew up in.

The world I grew up in had cheaper houses, cheaper college, and a dollar that bought more. The world you are growing up in does not. That is not your fault. It is not something you did wrong. It is a system that was built before you were born, and it is my job to make sure you understand it well enough to navigate it.

I care about this because I care about you. It is that simple.

Close

What comes next

You know more now than most people will ever learn about money.

That is not a boast on your behalf. It is an indictment of what passes for financial education in this country. Most Americans graduate from high school, college, even graduate school without ever being told that the dollar has lost ninety-five percent of its purchasing power in their grandparents' lifetime. They are taught to save, to invest, to diversify, to contribute to their 401(k), and to trust the system. Nobody tells them the system has a leak.

Now you know about the leak. The question is what you do with that knowledge.

The first thing you do is have the conversation. With your children. With your spouse. With your parents, if they are open to it. With the other parent at the birthday party, the one standing near the cooler, the one who has been feeling that something is wrong with the economy but has never been able to name it.

You can name it now. The money is losing its value because the people who control the money supply have every incentive to expand it and no effective constraint preventing them from doing so. That is not a conspiracy. It is a structure. It has been operating for over a century, and it is accelerating.

You do not need to convince anyone. You do not need to argue. You just need to say the thing plainly, the way this book has tried to say it, and let the other person decide what to do with it. Some will listen. Some will not. That is their right. Your job is not to convert anyone. Your job is to make sure your own children understand what they are inheriting.

The second thing you do is continue learning. This book is an introduction, not an encyclopedia. There are people who have spent years thinking about the subjects covered in these chapters, and their work is worth your time.

For the history of money and the case for sound money, read Saifedean Ammous, The Bitcoin Standard. It is the most thorough treatment of monetary history written for a general audience, and it builds the case for Bitcoin as the logical successor to gold. It is dense in places. It is worth the effort.

For the broader economic argument, read Jeff Booth, The Price of Tomorrow. Booth makes the case that technology is inherently deflationary, that our monetary system is designed to fight deflation with money creation, and that the collision between these two forces is the defining economic tension of our time. It is the clearest articulation of the argument made in Chapter 7 of this book.

For a clear-eyed explanation of how the monetary system actually works, watch or read anything by Lyn Alden. Her essay "How Money and Banking Work (and How They Break)" is the single best piece of financial education available to a general audience. If you read one thing after finishing this book, make it that.

For the human rights case for Bitcoin, read Alex Gladstein, Check Your Financial Privilege. Gladstein shows what happens when people in countries with collapsing currencies, authoritarian governments, and frozen bank accounts get access to money that nobody controls. It reframes Bitcoin from a first-world investment thesis to a tool of survival for billions of people. It will change the way you think about what money means to people who do not have the luxury of taking it for granted.

For a concise and beautifully written explanation of why Bitcoin matters, read Jimmy Song, Thank God for Bitcoin. It comes at the subject from a moral and philosophical angle, and it complements the economic argument with a deeper question: what kind of money is compatible with a just society?

If you want to go further, here are three principles for navigating the information landscape around Bitcoin.

First: ignore the price. The price of Bitcoin on any given day is noise. The signal is the network. Is it still running? Is the ledger still intact? Is the twenty-one million limit still in place? If the answer to all three is yes, the technology is working. The price will do what the price does. Your job is to understand the technology, not to trade the volatility.

Second: be skeptical of anyone selling you something. The Bitcoin ecosystem is full of people who want your money, your attention, or both. Influencers, trading platforms, altcoin promoters, newsletter writers promising ten-thousand-percent returns. Ignore them. Bitcoin does not need a sales pitch. If someone is selling you hard on a Bitcoin-related product, ask yourself who benefits from the sale. If the answer is not you, walk away.

Third: use multiple sources. Do not take this book's word for anything. Verify the claims. Look up the debt figures. Check the purchasing power charts. Read the opposing arguments. The best defense against being wrong is being willing to hear the other side. If the case for Bitcoin is as strong as I believe it is, it can survive your skepticism. If it cannot, you should not hold it.

There is one more thing, and then I am done.

I started this book with my father's diploma. MIT, 1947. Four hundred dollars. Two hundred hours of washing test tubes. That was the deal.

My children will not get that deal. Your children will not get that deal. The deal changed, and it changed because the money changed, and the money changed because the people who controlled it chose to change it, slowly enough that most people never noticed.

This book exists so that your children notice.

Not so they are angry. Not so they are afraid. So they are prepared. So they understand the system they are living inside, the way a sailor understands the weather: not to control it, but to navigate it. To know when the wind is shifting. To know where the rocks are. To know what to do when the storm comes.

The storm is not coming. The storm has been here for a century. Your grandparents sailed through the early part, when the wind was gentle. Your parents sailed through the middle, when the swells were getting bigger. Your children are sailing into the part where the waves are tall enough to see.

Give them the chart. Give them the compass. Give them the conversation.

And if they ask you what money is, you will know what to say.

A stone is worth the journey that it took.

A stone is known by every eye that looked.

No one can take what everyone remembers.

The ledger lives in us like light in embers.

www.ingramcontent.com/pod-product-compliance
Lightning Source LLC
LaVergne TN
LVHW050936210926
848482LV00013B/635
* 9 7 9 8 9 9 6 1 0 5 8 1 6 *